HOW TO SET UP

A

KINDLE FIRE

HD

The Ultimate Guide For Complete
Beginners On How to Setup a Kindle Fire
HD In 5 Minutes.

BY

DAVE BRUCE

Copyright©2018

COPYRIGHT

TABLE OF CONTENT

CHAPTER 1 ....**4**

   INTRODUCTION 4

CHAPTER 2 ....**6**

   HOW TO SETUP A KINDLE FIRE HD...............6

CHAPTER 3 ....**13**

   GET AMAZON CONNECTED 13

CHAPTER 4 ....**22**

   MAKING USE OF THE KINDLE FIRE HD 22

THE END **32**

CHAPTER 1

INTRODUCTION

The Kindle Fire HD is one of the world most popular android tablet with over 3 million users who owns it, with the amazing features it has in it.

Apart from the popular use of kindle fire device as an E-reader, it can also perform other functions. The user interface is a friendly one and it has a lot of good stuff in it.

This guide will show you how you can setup your Kindle Fire, all you have to do is just follow the steps as instructed. There are unlimited apps from other sources that can be setup in your kindle fire tablet, but if you find this very difficult, there is no needs to worry because I got you cover.

All over the world millions of people haven't been able to use and perform wonders with its features but dis book gives the breakdown of all solution to any problem you might encounter.

Thankfully each steps are very easy and simple to follow, that even a beginner can master it in a few minutes.

CHAPTER 2

HOW TO SETUP A KINDLE FIRE HD

Kindle Fire HD, which is also known as the Fire HD, is from Amazon's line of touchscreen tablet computers. Base on the differences between processor, screen size, and other features, and depending on the year of production for your Fire HD, these devices can be use for work, travel, etc. But its overall functions always remain unchanged.

Before begin using or setup your Fire HD apps to browser, read, view emails and other functions, first your Kindle Amazon need to be register with the help of the internet.

To do this follow the steps below:

First you have to Connect to the Internet:

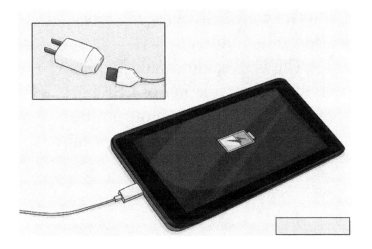

1. **Get your Kindle battery charged.**

The power adapters for your Kindle are sold separately, but can charge your Fire HD faster than a USB cable, although, your Kindle would come with a USB cable which will enable you connect your new device to a computer or a USB charging port to start charging.

Charge your Fire HD by:
→ Get your USB charger connected into your Kindle.
→ The USB cable should be plug into a power adapter or USB port.
→ Wait until your Kindle notifies you of full charged when the orange charging light turns green.

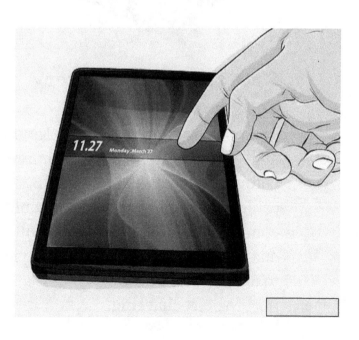

2. Immediately after full charge you should access the Welcome wireless connection screen.

Press the power button at the bottom of your Fire HD to turn it on from being off. Then you will see:

→ A slide bar that you will tap, hold and drag right which will enable you unlock your Kindle.

→ A "welcome" note, followed by available Wi-Fi networks. You should type your password and tap the OK button after selecting your network.

3. Changing Wi-Fi setting.

You may decide to obtain a new Wi-Fi network by moving your finger from top of the screen downwards, then type the network name and password to access it.

4. Troubleshoot Wi-Fi problems, when necessary.

Contact your internet provider if other devices can access your wireless network but your Kindle can't. Before doing this, try these common fixes for connectivity problems:

→ Turn Airplane mode off by dragging your finger from the top of your screen to the bottom, click the "wireless" option, and then click "Off" if Airplane mode is turn on.

→ By resetting Wi-Fi connection all you have to do is move your finger on the screen top down, select wireless — Wi-Fi — Off. Then tap "On".

→ To restart your Fire HD just tap the power button and hold it, remove your finger immediately it start. You can the power button again to set it on if Fire HD doesn't restart.

→ If you are unable to access your network amongst other networks, just position your device close to the router and select wireless → Wi-Fi, then tap "Scan".

CHAPTER 3

GET AMAZON CONNECTED

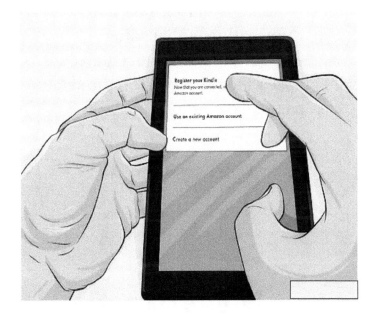

1. You have to continue your Kindle page registration.

Immediately after finish connecting your Kindle to your wireless network, "Kindle page Registration" should be prompted to appear on your screen. On this page you should see these:

→ "Enter Amazon Account Information" subheading.

→ Your password and email entry boxes should appear on the same page.

2. Type your Amazon account information or create an account.

If you already got Amazon account to proceed with the Fire HD, just type your email and password. Enter create account if you don't have towards the bottom of the screen.

→ failure to register your Kindle, you will be unable to access, purchase, or receive items through Amazon's Kindle store.

→ In other to buy content from Amazon you will need link your Amazon account to your preferred source of payment. Your credit card information for your Amazon account will be needed.

3. Agree to terms and conditions.

Select "Register" after reading through the terms and condition for using Kindle Fire HD and agreeing to it.

4. Your time zone should be set.

A page should appear with a heading "Select Your Time Zone" after registration with list of other time zones in the USA. At the bottom of the screen, select "More" if you live in another country to select your time zone.

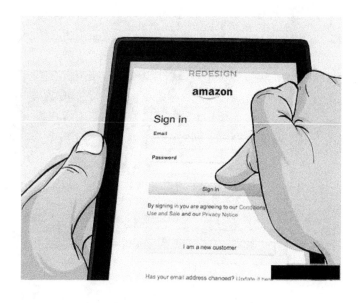

5. Confirming your account.

If accidentally you enter another account information instead of your account information, click the link to input and confirm your account.

6. Get your Kindle account link to your social media if you want.

You can link your Kindle account to social media like Facebook and twitter (optional).

To do this simply:

→ Select the social media that you desire.

→ Input your account information, such as your email and password.

→ Tap, <u>Get Started Now.</u>

7. With the tutorial, acquaint yourself with Fire HD features.

Using the tutorial, you can get acquainted with Fire HD features of your new device. This can be done by scrolling to the user's guide in your Kindle Fire HD Docs library.

CHAPTER 4

MAKING USE OF THE KINDLE FIRE HD

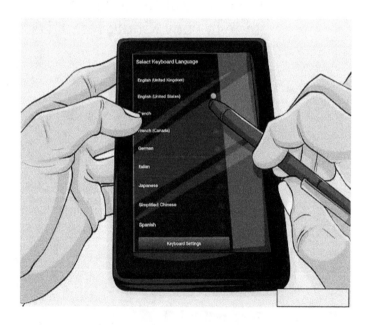

1. If you want, change your language settings.

To change your language setting, this can be done by moving your finger downward from the top of your screen. This should show a menu containing "Settings." Tap this and:

→ Tap "Keyboard and Language" from the options listed.
→ Select "Language".
→ Choose your language from the resulting list of languages.
→ From the "Language and Keyboard" menu change your keyboard language by tapping "Current Keyboard". After that select "Keyboard Language" → "Use System Language", and manually select your keyboard.
→ Select "Fire Keyboard" to choose your desire language if need to download a new keyboard for your language arise.

2. Manage your billing settings and account information.

Unlock your Kindle Fire HD by swiping your finger or inputting your password, also remove your Kindle Fire HD from sleep mode by tapping the button at the bottom of your Kindle.

From your home screen:

→ Choose "Manage Your Content and Devices."

→ Under the "Digital Payment Settings" option, choose the option titled "Edit Payment Method".

→ Next thing to do is to make adjustment enter your new payment information or your current payment method.

→ After updating your information completely, Select "Continue".

→ Once your Kindle redirects you to the "Digital Payment Settings" page confirm your information is correct.

3. Search your library for eBooks and other media you've already purchased.

Tap the Home icon to turn to the home screen, which will contain your content libraries. It is an icon shaped like a little house.

→ At this point all you need to do is select your desired content library to open your library of eBooks, but if you just setup your Amazon account, your content libraries will be totally empty.

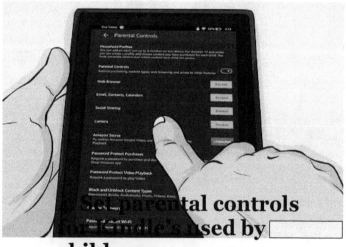

4. Setup parental controls for Kindle's used by children.

Swipe down from the top of the screen which will open your settings, there should be a "More" option. Tap it and then tap "Parental Settings" and:

→ To protect parental control settings for the Fire HD, tap "On", Which will prompt a request for a password. Type and confirm parental control password.

→ Next after a list of features appear that you can restrict. Select "On" for each feature that you wish restricted. Then tap "Finish."

→ To indicate Parental Control are enabled, you will see a small lock icon on the top status of your Kindle.

5. If you wish you can change your default browser search engine.

If you should prefer a different browser, such as Yahoo or Google, you can change it through your menu options. Enter your browser by selecting "Web" from the home screen, then tap the menu icon represented by three vertical dots.

→ Select "search engine" by moving to "Settings".

→ Select the search engine you want.

→ You can start browsing websites with your Kindle Fire HD.

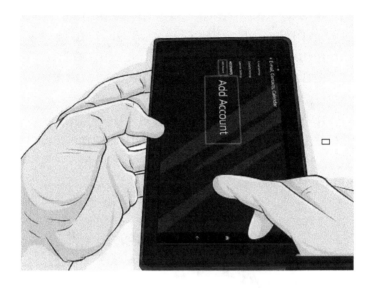

5. Confirm and setup your email.

On the home screen select the house icon. After that, you should select "Apps" and select the "Mail" mail icon. When you see of list common email services, select one and follow the prompt or input your email information.

→ To link your email account to your Kindle Fire HD, input your email and password.

7. Run experiment with other apps.

To locate potential services and features that personalize your Kindle Fire HD to your preference. Select the home icon → Apps → Store to open the Amazon Appstore.

→ To purchase most apps in the appstore will cost money so remember to check the cost of the app before purchasing.

Thank you for reading my book, you can check out my other books below.

HOW DO I SIDELOAD APPS INTO MY KINDLE FIRE

HOW TO SET UP YOUR AMAZON ECHO – DAVE BRUCE

HOW TO SET UP YOUR NEW CHROMECAST – WILLIAMS ROGUE

HOW DO I INSTALL GOOGLE PLAY ON KINDLE FIRE – DAVE BRUCE

THE END

www.ingramcontent.com/pod-product-compliance
Lightning Source LLC
La Vergne TN
LVHW052324060326
832902LV00023B/4589